Living Love Forward

Kill 'em With Kindness

A Children's Leadership Series

Written by Kim Dawson

Illustrated by Paige Anocibar

Publisher: Tandem Services Press
PO Box 220, Yucaipa, CA 92399
www.tandemservicesink.com

Book Design by Paige Anocibar

ISBN 978-1-954986-25-1

Appreciation to

Inland Leaders Charter School and all our teachers and staff for inspiring and supporting me to write this series.

All my students and their families who taught me to be a better teacher and person.

The 2nd, 3rd, 4th, and 5th grade classes at Inland Leaders that gave me GREAT feedback, which strengthened my story.

Pelican Elementary in Oregon for letting us use their school as a model for Lexie's Huckleberry Elementary.

Leanne Cullen at Pelican Elementary for inspiring me to create a new character (Mrs. Carlton, the lunch lady).

Ruth Chamberlin for letting me borrow her artwork for the hallways of Huckleberry Elementary (Pelican mural).

My family and friends who have never wavered in supporting and encouraging my mission to help others.

Paige, my illustrator, for putting up with my "creative" tangents.

Jennifer Crosswhite, my editor and friend, who has been my sounding board and always keeps me positive when I hit the many bumps in the road. (https://www.tandemservicesink.com)

All my readers who have supported me and helped me spread the message that kids can be leaders too.

Sending a ton of love and encouragement to all of you!
We got this!

From the author of the series Living Love Forward:

I wrote this children's leadership series to create an open conversation about the experiences our kids face every day. Being a teacher for over two decades, I have created connections with kids of all ages. I have observed and learned a lot through these interactions and have discovered key skill sets that I think are important for their growth. My purpose in writing these sentimental and caring stories is the hope that they instill life skills and resilience in our children. In turn, this empowers them to become successful, compassionate, and strong leaders. Join Lexie and our children as they navigate this journey of self-discovery.

Please note that this series can be used in conjunction with any Leadership Program focused on survival skills and effective habits for children.

This book specifically focuses on:

- **Bullying**
- **Lack of social skills**
- **Confrontation**
- **Name calling**
- **Negative attitude**
- **Poor coping skills**
- **Poor self-esteem**
- **Poor peer relation**

Map of Harlow

Train Station

Church Of Hope

Cemetery

Liberty Library

Lexie's House

Bus Stop

1st Street
2nd Street
2nd Street
Rise Road
Daisy Lane
4th Street
Main St
Main Street
Main Street

Jackson Sports Park

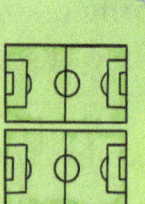

Lavendar Lane
Lotus Loop
Lavendar Lane
Jasmine Avenue
Jasmine Avenue
Jasmine Avenue
Rose Road

Riverside Park

Annabelle's House

Huckleberry Elementary
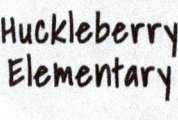

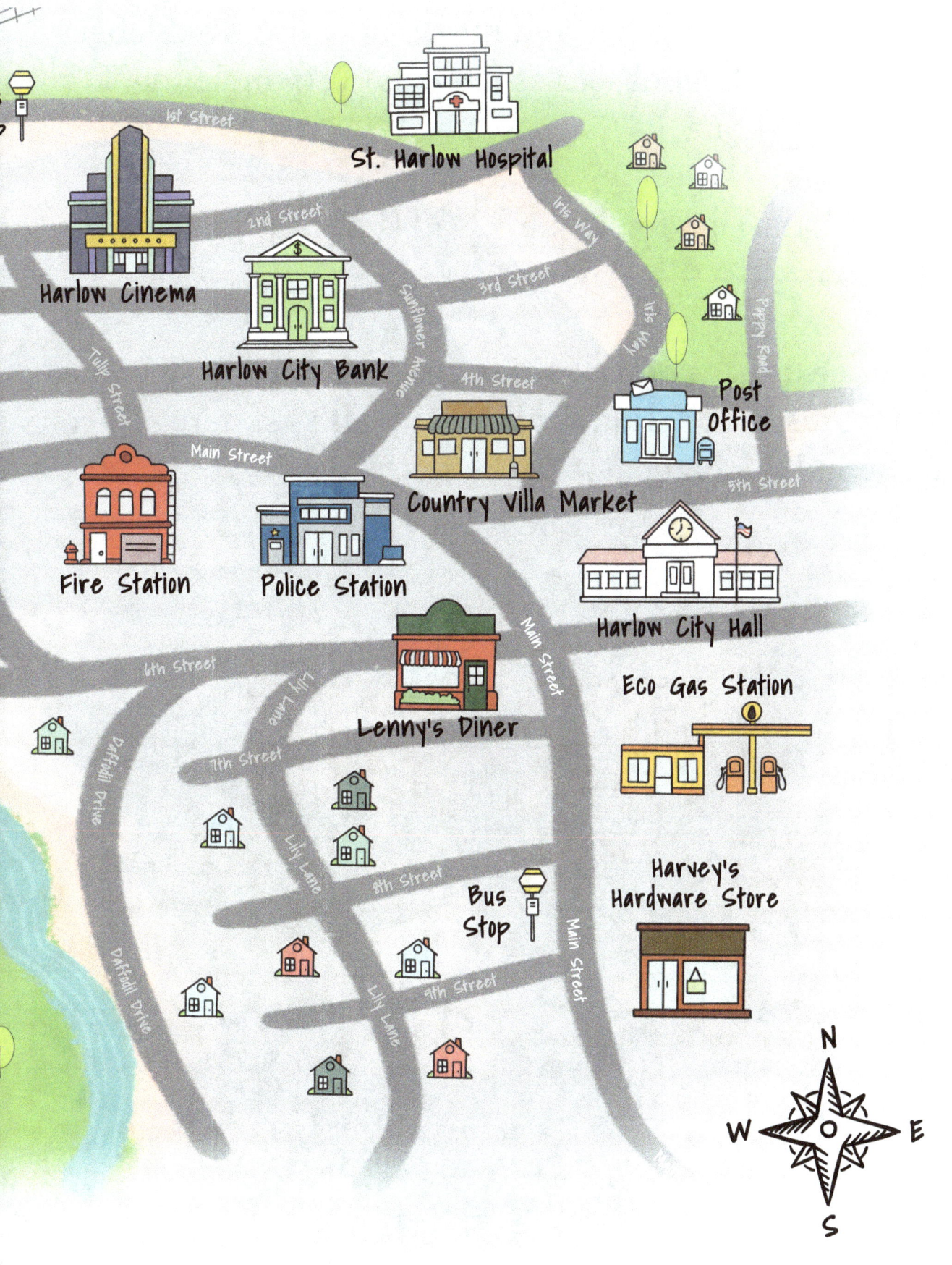

Dad drops my brother and me off near the Huckleberry Elementary School sign as he does every morning. I sigh as I get out.

"What's the sigh for, Lexie?" Dad shouts as I go to close the door.

I glance back at him, "I am so ready for Friday to come, Dad. I just want Friday to hurry up and get here so I can go spend the night at Annabelle's.

"It's Thursday at least," he says, "Hang in there, kiddo! Try and turn that mood around or else today will drag out even more. Find something that makes you feel good and your mood will go from being upset to being happier. That always helps me."

I try to do what Dad suggested and I notice that the morning passes quickly and soon we get excused to go to lunch. I hurry to the lunch line and wait patiently for my turn.

My stomach is growling. I should have had that toast Dad wanted me to eat this morning. I wasn't hungry then, but I definitely regret not taking at least a couple of bites like he suggested. "Hurry! Hurry!" I chant in my head.

Finally, I get up to the front of the line and Mrs. Carlton, our lunch lady, asks me if I want, salad, spaghetti or one of the bagged lunches today. I really like Mrs. Carlton. She is always smiling and is always nice to everyone.

She is an awesome cook too and spaghetti is my favorite, so I can't help myself and say, "Spaghetti please with a smile on top!"

This makes Mrs. Carlton laugh and she gives me some extra meat sauce. I giggle and say thank you as I leave to go find Annabelle.

I spot her sitting at the back table and proceed to go sit with her. "I saved you a spot," she says as I get closer. Annabelle always makes me feel better. She is my very best friend.

"I am starving today!" I exclaim. I start eating as soon as my tray hits the table. Annabelle starts to laugh as she continues to eat her lunch.

"Are you still coming over tomorrow to spend the night?" she asks.

Glancing at her over my fork full of spaghetti, I tell her that I am definitely coming over and that I can't wait to go on her new trampoline. I tell her that Dad will be off from his shift by four o'clock and he will bring me over after. She is nodding while I am sharing, just as excited as I am for Friday to get here.

Riiiiiiing!

Mrs. Bryce, my teacher, looks up from the pile of papers she is grading and tells us to clean up, stack our chairs, grab our jackets, and we are dismissed for the day. Music to my ears, as I rush to get everything done and head out the door to go home.

I am ready by the time Dad gets home. He asks me about my day as we amble to the car. Dad looks tired. I think he has had a rough and long week too. I can only see the back of his head as we drive, so I call out his name, look at him in the rearview mirror when he glances up, and I say, "I love you, Dad."

He turns his head towards me and says, "I needed that, kiddo. I love you too."

We pass over the bridge and drive by Riverside Park. It doesn't take us long to get to Annabelle's house. As we pull into Annabelle's driveway, I grab my bag ready to launch out of the car. I do just that when we stop. Dad just laughs and yells out, "Have a great time, Sweetheart. I will come to get you tomorrow after my shift is over. Love you."

I smile at him through the window, wave goodbye, and blow him a kiss. I race across the grass to the front door. Annabelle is waiting for me, and she waves goodbye to my dad as he leaves.

We race up the stairs to her bedroom, throw my bags on the floor, run through her house to the backyard, and play on her trampoline until dinner. Annabelle's mom calls out for us to go wash up and we meet at the table.

We eat and talk throughout dinner. At one point, her mom asks us how school is going. Annabelle mentions some mean things that kids are doing at recess. Annabelle's mom asks us what we do when kids are mean to us.

I look at Annabelle and we both shrug our shoulders. We aren't sure how to answer her question. I finally answer with, "Well, we usually go tell a teacher or yard duty, when someone is being mean, but that doesn't always help. The kids are still mean behind the adults' backs."

Annabelle's mom nods and then says, "Have you ever tried to kill 'em with kindness?"

Annabelle and I look at each other in confusion. I don't know what that means. I can tell from the look on Annabelle's face that she is clueless too.

Her mom and dad both notice our confusion. They look at each other as if trying to figure out how to help us understand what kill 'em with kindness means. They try to describe it to us, but we don't understand. We just get more confused. Eventually, they decide to act it out and demonstrate what kill 'em with kindness "looks like" using examples that happen with kids at school.

Annabelle's dad says, "Ok, I am going to pretend to be the mean kid at school and Mom is going to be the kid being bullied or picked on." Her dad turns to Annabelle's mom and says in a snotty voice, "Why are you wearing that shirt? It looks terrible on you!" Annabelle's mom smiles a sweet smile and responds, "It's a nice day today. I hope you have a super one too!" Both Annabelle and I are still confused.

Her dad tries to explain again. He shares that when you switch the mean conversation to something different and say something kind instead, it makes the person being mean pause. They pause because they don't know how to respond or react to what you just said. They don't know what to say because you didn't respond the way they thought you would. This usually makes them stop being mean and move on. If it doesn't stop them from being mean, then you keep doing it until they stop. "The trick is for you NOT to get upset." he continues.

Her parents try another example. This time her mom is the mean kid and Annabelle's dad is the kid being picked on. She says, "I don't think we should be friends anymore! You are a terrible person!"

Annabelle's dad calmly responds to her, "You sound like you are having a rough day. I hope it gets better for you. Take care of yourself!"

This time Mom is the mean kid and Dad is the kid being picked on.

I don't think we should be friends anymore! You are a terrible person!

You sound like you are having a rough day. I hope it gets better for you. Take care of yourself!

He pauses and looks at us for a second and then says. "After this, you simply just walk away. They don't know what to say to you because they thought you would respond by being upset or getting your feelings hurt. Now,...you might be really upset that they don't want to be friends anymore. That part is hard and can hurt your feelings. Just know that in killing 'em with kindness, you shut the mean conversation down and they can't continue to pick on you. This is just something extra you can do to take care of yourself, but it is still important to tell an adult what is happening," he concludes.

Mom smiles and says, "Ok, you girls try. Annabelle, why don't you start and be the mean kid and Lexie you can be the kid being picked on"

Annabelle starts by saying, "Lexie, you stink and I don't want to sit by you!" I think for a second and then tell her, "That's not a nice thing to say. I think there is a seat open near Cindy. I can go sit over there. I hope you have a better day!" Her parents smile and nod their heads in encouragement.

Mom says, "That's perfect! You didn't get upset by what she said, you said something kind to her, and then you found a way to get away from the kid being mean. Excellent!"

It's my turn to be the mean kid. I turn to Annabelle and say, "I don't like you! No one wants to be your friend!"

Annabelle thinks for a second like I did and smiling she says, "I like your shoes. They go nicely with your outfit."

Everyone pauses at the table and then we all start laughing. It isn't what any of us expected her to say, which makes it so funny. We continue eating and chatting about other kinds of things to say to people who are being mean. However, we all agree that Annabelle's shoe comeback was the best one out of all of them!

Monday comes around and Dad drives us to school. When we arrive, I jump out of the car knowing it is going to be a better week. I feel happy. As I approach the school, I notice Jason, one of the kids who bullies a lot, standing next to the school sign as we walk past it. He yells, "Hey, where is your stupid grey hat? You wear it every week. You are such a weirdo?" Then he chuckles with his friends waiting for me to respond.

I take a breath, look at him, and say, "It's a beautiful day today, Jason. I hope that your day gets better and you stop picking on kids. Oh, and I like your shoes." I smile when I notice the confused look on Jason's face and continue walking.

The morning flies by and soon it is time for lunch. I follow my class to the lunch line. This time my stomach isn't growling as badly. When I get to the front of the line, I notice that the boy in front of me is saying mean things to Mrs. Carlton as she helps him get his lunch. It is obvious she is getting frustrated with him.

"Who is mean to Mrs. Carlton? This is not ok!" I think to myself. I turn to her and whisper loud enough so she can hear me. I say, "kill 'em with kindness, Mrs. C!"

She looks at me for a moment as if trying to comprehend what I am telling her. Then she smiles and I know she understands. She is an adult and figures out what it means faster than Annabelle and I did. She leans towards the boy having a rough day and who is being mean and says, "Stanley, I think you are a great kid and maybe having a bad day. I hope it turns around for you and gets better."

I move to the next spot in line and grab my lunch. She turns to me and whispers, "kill 'em with kindness...I will remember that!"

Mrs. Carlton gives me a wink and a smile as I walk on by.

Author's Advice

• Know your "kill 'em with kindness" phrase so you are ready if someone starts to be mean to you (examples: Wow! You look really pretty today! Or is that a new shirt you are wearing? It looks good on you!).

• If someone is picking on you many times a day or week, make sure to tell an adult so they can help.

• It is okay to have a voice and stand up for yourself when someone is picking on you.

• Kill 'em with kindness is just another strategy to use when someone is not treating you kindly.

• You are worth knowing, you are a gift to the people you meet, and KNOW that you don't deserve to have mean things said to you just because someone else is struggling.

Think and Feel

What would you say to someone if you were going to "kill 'em with kindness?"

Please Note: When someone is being mean to you it is common to not be able to think of what to say. If you have your "kill 'em with kindness" phrase already figured out beforehand, then you just say that. It is supposed to stop the conversation, so it is okay if it is a bit random and silly like Annabelle's . Once you have it in your head, share it with someone and find out what theirs is.

Glossary

amble

Definition: to walk at a slow, easy pace

Part of Speech:

This word is a (noun, adjective, verb, adverb).

Evidence of how the word is used in the story.

Dad and Lexie amble (walk slowly) to their car when it is time for him to drop her off at Annabelle's house for their sleepover.

clueless

Definition: having absolutely no understanding, awareness, or knowledge of something

Part of Speech:

This word is a (noun, adjective, verb, adverb).

Evidence of how the word is used in the story.

At first, both Lexie and Annabelle are clueless (not understanding) of what kill 'em with kindness means.

Glossary

comprehend

Definition: to understand or grasp the meaning of

Part of Speech:

This word is a (noun, adjective, verb, adverb).

Evidence of how the word is used in the story.

Lexie gets upset with a boy being mean to Mrs.Carlton and she tells her to kill him with kindness. Mrs. Carlton looks confused and then comprehends (understands) what Lexie is saying.

launch

Definition: to jump, send, or shoot something into the air with great force

Part of Speech:

This word is a (noun, adjective, verb, adverb).

Evidence of how the word is used in the story.

When Dad stops the car in front of Annabelle's house, Lexie launches herself (she jumps) out of the car, because she is excited to be there.

Glossary

Music to my ears

Definition: something that someone is very happy to hear

Language Usage:

"Music to my ears" is an idiom
(An idiom is a phrase that means something different than the literal words being used. Examples: "It is raining cats and dogs" means it is raining very hard and "Go break a leg!" means go try your hardest)

Evidence of how the word is used in the story.

When the bell rings, signaling it is time to go home, it is music to her ears (she was very happy to hear the bell ring) because she wants to go home.

pause

Definition: to stop for a short time

Part of Speech:

This word is a (noun, adjective, verb, adverb).

Evidence of how the word is used in the story.

Annabelle's parents explain that when you kill someone with kindness you cause them to pause (stop for a short time in confusion) because they are expecting you to be upset by their meanness.

Glossary

proceed

Definition: to begin or go on to do something; to move forward after a stop

Part of Speech:

This word is a (noun, adjective, verb, adverb).

Evidence of how the word is used in the story.

Lexie gets her lunch and proceeds (goes towards, moves forward) to the lunch area to find Annabelle.

trampoline

Definition: a sheet of strong canvas attached to a frame by springs. Trampolines are used for jumping and tumbling

Part of Speech:

This word is a (noun, adjective, verb, adverb).

Evidence of how the word is used in the story.

Lexie can't wait to go to Annabelle's house and play on her new trampoline.

About the Author: Kim Dawson

I am a single mom of two wonderful kids. I have been teaching for a number of decades and love spending time with my students. I have been writing since I was a child. It has always been a way for me to express myself when I am struggling. I strongly believe that we do not give our kids the credit they deserve. They have a lot to teach us if we just listen.

About the Illustrator: Paige Anocibar

Art is my passion. Every day I am thankful to have a career that empowers me to express myself through creativity. Drawing has been a part of my life since I was a small child. Coloring and painting were my favorite part of going to school. Back then, just like now, I was eager for the next art project. I knew that expressing myself through art is all I have ever wanted to do with my life, and illustrating this book has helped me achieve a part of that dream.

If you enjoyed this story, see other books in this Children's Leadership series, Living Love Forward.

2023 Books

February   May   September   November

2024 Books

February   May   September   November